You Are Like a Seed
Text Copyright ©2019 by Michaun Madsen
Illustrations Copyright ©2019 by Alyssa de Asis

ISBN: 978-087516-902-6
Library of Congress Catalog Card Number: 2018962658
Second Edition, 2020

Printed in Canada

DeVorss & Company, Publishers
PO Box 1389
Camarillo CA 93011-1389
www.devorss.com

A seed is a tiny little miracle.

Inside a seed is everything it will need
to grow into exactly what it is *meant* to be!

You are like a seed.
Inside of you is every single thing you need to
be exactly who you are *meant* to be!

When you plant a seed and surround it with good soil and water, something special happens. The seed absorbs the healthy nutrients and gets stronger as it struggles to work and grow, until one day . . .

. . . out pops a tiny little sprout.

You are like a seed.

You are surrounded by a loving family in your home where you will eat healthy food, drink plenty of water, and absorb nourishing lessons as you struggle to work and grow.

But, the seed is *just beginning.*
It still has more to do.

The little seed must reach and climb with
all its might so it can absorb more light and
turn it into energy to grow even bigger.

You are like a seed.
You must also reach and climb with all your might
as you grow bigger and stronger. The knowledge, light,
and truth that you absorb becomes your energy.

The most beautiful part of a seed
is hidden inside where you can't see.
One day the seed will unfold its inner beauty.
It may be a sunflower, an apple tree,
or even a palm tree.

As the seed gets bigger and
grows fruit, or shady leaves,
or pretty flowers, it also does something
very special: it makes others happy . . .
just by being *itself!*

You are like a seed.
As you grow and your true self unfolds,
you will also make others happy because
you are also just being *yourself.*
It's that simple!

In nature, everything has its own purpose. A scratchy weed feeds an insect . . .

a huckleberry bush grows fruit for a pie . . .

a giant redwood tree has strong limbs
to hold a nest. Each teeny tiny seed has a
special purpose that will guide it forever.

You are like a seed.

As you continue to grow, you will begin to see your inner beauty unfold. You may become a musician, a doctor, a teacher, a parent or whatever you find inside of you. Your life will serve a purpose.

Each and every different seed makes
the world a wonderful and exciting place
because of its special purpose.

The acorn from an oak tree is not meant
to be a watermelon, nor is the carrot seed
meant to be a grape vine. Just imagine what
the world would be like if we never had
a carrot or a grape seed.

You are like a seed.

You were not meant to be someone else.

YOU were meant to be YOU . . .

which is exactly what the world needs.

So relax and soak in the sunlight.
There may be some struggling as you reach
and climb, but that's OK. It's all part of
an amazing journey . . .

. . . The journey to become you!